All Is Bright

Visit Tyndale online at www.tyndale.com.

Visit Tyndale Momentum online at www.tyndalemomentum.com.

Tyndale Momentum and the Tyndale Momentum logo are registered trademarks of Tyndale House Publishers, Inc. Tyndale Momentum is an imprint of Tyndale House Publishers, Inc., Carol Stream, IL.

All Is Bright: A Devotional Journey to Color Your Way to Christmas

Devotional text taken from *Let Every Heart Prepare Him Room*, published in 2010 by Tyndale House Publishers, Inc., under ISBN 978-1-4143-6441-4.

Designed by Beth Sparkman

Printed in China

21   20   19   18   17   16

6   5   4   3   2   1

All is Bright

A devotional journey to color your way to Christmas

WRITTEN BY **Nancy Guthrie**

ILLUSTRATED BY **Lizzie Preston**

TYNDALE MOMENTUM

An Imprint of Tyndale House Publishers, Inc.

LIVING EXPRESSIONS™ COLLECTION

Introduction

As December dawns, most families are busy putting Christmas programs and parties on the calendar, making holiday travel plans, and purchasing gifts. Those are all wonderful things, but it's important to nurture a longing in our hearts and our homes for a fresh sense of wonder that God has come to us in Jesus.

As you enter into this Christmas season, I hope this book will remind you of how God's people longed for centuries for the Messiah to come. *All Is Bright* provides a short reading for every day in the month of December, as well as a beautiful accompanying coloring page, taking you on a creative journey of identifying with the distant longings of Israel, listening for the angel's announcement, and gazing at the Baby in the manger. In the back of this book, you'll also find the Family Activities section, which includes kid-friendly coloring pages and conversation questions for your whole family that will help transform this season into a meaningful time of devotion and discussion as you focus together on what God's Word says about the promise of Christ.

The busyness of December can easily crowd out contemplation of the amazing reality of God's coming to live among us as one of us. I hope that your family will overcome the empty busyness of this season and that all will be bright with the glory of Jesus.

Nancy Guthrie

The Promised One

When someone promises us something wonderful, we can hardly wait for that promise to be fulfilled. If the promise is something good, we want it *now*! We really don't like to wait. And yet the very best things are worth waiting for.

A long, long time ago, God made a promise to his people, Israel. In fact, he made many promises to them. But God's most important promise—the promise all his other promises depended on—was that he would send the Messiah, the Anointed One, who would save them from the difficulties of living life in this world broken by sin. The Messiah would not be an ordinary person, but God's own Son. The people he made the promise to had to wait, putting all their faith in the One who made the promise.

The season leading up to Christmas is called Advent, which means *coming*. During Advent, we remember the thousands of years God's chosen people anticipated and longed for the coming of God's salvation through the Messiah. Then, at Christmas, we celebrate the fulfillment of the promises God made. Jesus—the Savior God had promised—was born to us. No more waiting. Jesus came.

When John the Baptist was born, his father, Zechariah, recognized that the long years of waiting were finally over. God gave him a special understanding that his son, John, was going to prepare the way for the promised Messiah. Zechariah celebrated that God was about to fulfill his promise. He said, "Praise the Lord, the God of Israel, because he has visited and redeemed his people. He has sent us a mighty Savior from the royal line of his servant David, just as he promised through his holy prophets long ago" (Luke 1:68-70).

God promised that he would send a Savior, which he did when Jesus became a human baby. And while Jesus did everything necessary to save us when he came the first time, he also promised to come again. Then all God's promises will be completely fulfilled. So again we are waiting. Waiting patiently for God to fulfill his promises is what it means to have faith.

Putting faith in God's promises is not something a person does only one time on the day he or she becomes a Christian. The essence of being a Christian is placing all our hope in God, knowing we can trust him to fulfill all his promises—even the ones that haven't been fulfilled yet. We are willing to wait, trusting that "God's way is perfect. All the LORD's promises prove true" (Psalm 18:30).

DECEMBER 2

Right on Time

*M*ost days we set specific times for when we will go to school, have piano lessons, or get picked up from our friend's house. But sometimes there is not a specific time set for something, and we're left waiting, wondering when the package will be delivered, when the plumber will arrive at our house, or when our ride is going to show up. We wonder if we've been forgotten.

By the time Jesus was born, the Jewish people had been waiting for hundreds of years for God to send his promised Messiah. It had been more than four hundred years since they had even heard God speak to them through one of his prophets about the Savior he would send. It seemed like God had stopped talking to them, and some people had grown weary of keeping up their hopes that God would come through for them. While they were waiting, the Romans occupied their country and ruled over them. This made them long even more for the great Deliverer God had promised.

Though it is hard to wait on God, and though it sometimes seems to us that God is slow, God's timing is always perfect. He is never late. He always acts at just the right time.

God knew when the time was just right to send Jesus, the Messiah, into the world. He knew when the exact religious, cultural, and political conditions were in place. Paul wrote, "*When the right time came*, God sent his Son, born of a woman" (Galatians 4:4, emphasis added). You see, God is not making up plans as he goes. All the grand events of God's plan for our redemption have been scheduled in advance, from Creation to the enslavement and exodus of God's people from Egypt; to David's taking the throne in Israel; to the birth, death, and resurrection of Jesus; to the day when Jesus will return. Paul said that God "has set a day for judging the world" (Acts 17:31). The course and timing of history is not a mystery to God. Time is in his hands, and he will bring about his plans and purposes in our world and in our lives right on time.

Family Matters

You might know people who can trace their ancestors to someone famous—a war hero, an inventor, a sports legend, or a Hollywood actor. People who are related to someone famous usually like to talk about it, but it is different when people can trace their ancestry to someone infamous for being a liar or murderer or thief. Descendants of these kinds of people are not usually so quick to want to talk about their ancestor.

But that is not the case with Jesus. The Gospels of Matthew and Luke both include a genealogy—a record of Jesus' human ancestry—and it includes some people known more for terrible sin than for something good. Matthew began his book this way: "This is a record of the ancestors of Jesus the Messiah, a descendant of David and of Abraham . . ." The list goes on for many generations and ends, "Jacob was the father of Joseph, the husband of Mary. Mary gave birth to Jesus, who is called the Messiah" (Matthew 1:1, 16). Luke traced Jesus' ancestry all the way back to Adam, beginning, "Jesus was known as the son of Joseph," and ending, "Adam was the son of God" (Luke 3:23, 38).

When we look through the list of people in Jesus' ancestral line, we see people famous for their faith—like Noah and Abraham and David. But we also see people with tarnished reputations—like Judah, who was intimate with his daughter-in-law; Rahab, who was a Canaanite prostitute; and Manasseh, the king who put false idols in the Temple. Even Noah, Abraham, and David, as faithful as they were, were sinners, and all of them needed a Savior.

We find hope in the ancestry of Jesus that no matter what we've done or where we come from, we too can be included in Jesus' family. Jesus does not look for people who are perfect and have never failed or made mistakes to be in his family. Instead, he is drawn toward people who recognize their failures and see their need for him.

A SHOOT WILL COME UP
FROM THE STUMP OF JESSE;

FROM HIS ROOTS
A BRANCH WILL BEAR FRUIT.

ISAIAH 11:1, NIV

DECEMBER 4

Getting and Giving

This is the season our mailboxes are filled with stacks of mail-order catalogs, and the television is full of advertisements of all kinds of shiny new things wrapped up with red bows. Through their colorful pictures and creative words, advertisers seek to convince us that we don't have enough stuff—that we need more, newer, better. It is their job to convince us to feel dissatisfied and discontented with what we have. They want to feed our natural desires for more than we really need.

So how will our family respond to all the messages around us this time of year? How can we make sure that Christmas in our house is about more than making lists of the stuff we want and figuring out what to give to other people? Do we really need to keep collecting more stuff and spending more money on ourselves? Can we stop believing the lie that the more we get, the more satisfied we'll be?

By putting our focus on giving to others and meeting their very real needs, we can battle the greed in our hearts. Christmas is a season not of getting, but of giving, because at Christmas we are celebrating that God is the most generous and outrageous Giver in the universe. After all, he gave us his Son. Proverbs says, "Some people are always greedy for more, but the godly love to give!" (Proverbs 21:26). To pour ourselves into becoming outrageous givers is to pursue becoming more like God. God turns greedy, grasping, fearful hoarders into generous, honest, cheerful givers.

To become givers, we have to decide not to listen to the voice inside us that tells us we must keep a tight grip on what we have so we will never be in need. We have to reject the lie that money in the bank and a pantry full of food takes care of our needs, remembering that ultimately it is God who takes care of all our needs. We have to tell ourselves the truth about God—that because he has been so generous in giving us Jesus, we can be confident that he will give us everything we need. We take him at his word, believing that he can satisfy us and that he will bless us as we give to others. We trust his promise that "it is more blessed to give than to receive" (Acts 20:35).

DECEMBER 5

God Pitched His Tent

It can be great fun to put up a tent in your backyard to play in or sleep in. Imagine what it would be like for someone else to put up a tent in your backyard and begin living there—right in your backyard! In a sense, John says Jesus did just that. "So the Word became human and made his home among us" (John 1:14). The Greek word translated "made his home" is the word for "set up a tent." This verse is saying that God became a human person who set up his tent in our backyard and moved in.

If another family were to put up a tent in your backyard to live in, they would probably use your bathroom and have their meals around your table. They would be with you almost all the time, and no doubt their lives would intertwine with yours. This is what Jesus did when he became human. He made his home with us. He did this so that his life would be intertwined with ours—so that we would share our lives with him and so we could see him up close and really know him.

When we see God up close in the person of Jesus, what do we see? John wrote, "He was full of unfailing love and faithfulness" (John 1:14). Imagine having someone living with you who always loved perfectly and who was completely dependable to do what he said he would do. Doesn't that seem like the kind of person you would want to have making himself at home with your family?

John writes that many people of Jesus' day were not so happy to have Jesus right there with them. "He came to his own people, and even they rejected him. But to all who believed him and accepted him, he gave the right to become children of God" (John 1:11-12). While many rejected him, there were those who believed and accepted him. To believe and accept Jesus is to invite him to make his home with you and among you. It is to welcome him in, not as a guest, but as a permanent part of the family.

I Am the Lord's Servant

It's hard to imagine how frightening it must have been for teenage Mary to see an angel and hear him speaking to her. The Bible says that "Gabriel appeared to her and said, 'Greetings, favored woman! The Lord is with you!' Confused and disturbed, Mary tried to think what the angel could mean. 'Don't be afraid, Mary,' the angel told her, 'for you have found favor with God!'" (Luke 1:28-30). We can't help but wonder what the angel looked like and what he sounded like.

As frightening as it must have been to see and hear an angel speaking to her, it must have been even more frightening for Mary to process what the angel was telling her—that she was going to become pregnant, even though she had never been intimate with a man. This would be a scandal in her village. Everyone would whisper about her. She would be shunned and perhaps sent away by her fiancé, Joseph, because he would think she had been unfaithful to him. And yet, even though she probably had a million questions and concerns, Mary responded to the angel by welcoming whatever God wanted to do. She said, "I am the Lord's servant. May everything you have said about me come true" (Luke 1:38). In a sense she said to God, "I'm yours. You can do anything you want with me," even though she must have known that this situation would be very hard for her, for Joseph, and for her whole family.

It's easy to label what we consider "good things" in our lives as gifts from God and to welcome them with gratitude. But when difficult things happen, we don't look at them as part of God's good plan for us. Mary's example shows us we can also welcome those things we would not necessarily label "good," confident that God's gifts sometimes come in perplexing and even painful packages. When we belong to God, we know he will use whatever he allows into our lives for good. Somehow, in God's hands, these things also become gifts of his grace toward us.

It takes faith—faith to rest in who God is and his love for us; faith to be confident that he is doing something good in and through our difficult circumstances—to see the hard things in our lives as gifts of God's grace.

Name Him Jesus

Most parents spend a lot of time thinking about what they will name their babies. They think through names with special meanings, traditional family names, and names they just like.

It was common in the time when Jesus was born for parents to give their baby the name of someone in the family. But this is not what Mary and Joseph did. They didn't have to make a list of possibilities of what they might name the baby. An angel appeared separately to Mary and then to Joseph, telling each of them exactly what name to give the baby.

To Mary the angel said, "You will conceive and give birth to a son, and you will name him Jesus" (Luke 1:31). The angel also spoke to Joseph in a dream, saying, "Joseph, son of David . . . do not be afraid to take Mary as your wife. For the child within her was conceived by the Holy Spirit. And she will have a son, and you are to name him Jesus, for he will save his people from their sins" (Matthew 1:20-21).

The name *Jesus* was no random name, though it was an ordinary name for a Jewish boy in that day. The name *Jesus* was rich with meaning about who this child would be and what he would do.

Jesus (*Yeshua* in Hebrew) means "the LORD saves." It is a combination of *Yahu*, a personal name for God, and *shua*, which means "a cry for help" or "a saving cry." So by this name the angel was telling Joseph and Mary that this child would be a rescuer, a savior—someone who would prove to be no less than God himself in the body of a baby.

Jesus' very name tells us why he came and why his coming was such cause for celebration that we still celebrate his coming today. Jesus is "the LORD saves." He has come to rescue us from the sin that would keep us apart from God for eternity.

DECEMBER 8

He Will Be Very Great

People like to try to guess about babies even before they are born—boy or girl, shy or rambunctious, athletic or artful. But, of course, we don't know what a baby will be like until he or she is here.

While there were certainly many things Mary and Joseph did not know about the baby Mary was carrying, the angel Gabriel told them some amazing things about him. "He will be very great and will be called the Son of the Most High. The Lord God will give him the throne of his ancestor David. And he will reign over Israel forever; his Kingdom will never end!" (Luke 1:32-33). It must have been more than Mary could take in or understand.

The angel said that Jesus would be "very great." Who do you think is great? Whoever it is, Jesus is greater. All the smartest people of our day would have to sit at the feet of Jesus to learn from him. All the bravest military men of our day would want to follow behind him. All the greatest musicians would be hushed at the beauty of his music. Jesus is very great.

The angel Gabriel also said that Jesus "will be called the Son of the Most High." This is different from when God refers to the nation of Israel as his "firstborn son" (Exodus 4:22) and Christians as "sons of the Most High" (Luke 6:35, NIV). The angel was saying that Jesus would be *the* Son of the Most High God. This child would not be an ordinary person, but the one and only Son of God become human. Mary was carrying the Son of God inside her body!

Then Gabriel said, "The Lord God will give him the throne of his ancestor David." It might be hard for *us* to understand why this was a big deal, but Mary knew why. Her son was going to be a king—but not just any king. Jesus, a descendant of King David, would be the descendant whom God had promised hundreds of years before who would finally make things right for God's people. God had promised King David, "I will raise up one of your descendants, your own offspring, and I will make his kingdom strong. . . . I will secure his royal throne forever. . . . Your kingdom will continue before me for all time, and your throne will be secure forever" (2 Samuel 7:12-13, 16). Mary's baby would finally fulfill this promise!

Obviously this King would be different from all other kings, who come and go. Gabriel said, "He will reign over Israel forever; his Kingdom will never end!" *Never end?* Even now, King Jesus is on the throne of the universe. Though we can't see this with our eyes, we know it is true. But one day we *will* see it with our eyes, and every person will bow before King Jesus!

DECEMBER 9

Overshadowed

If you have ever driven through thick fog—so thick you could barely see what was in front of you—you know it can be kind of scary. Fog is basically a cloud close to the ground. In several places in the Bible, the presence and power of God in the person of the Holy Spirit is described as a cloud in which God came close to earth—but it usually didn't scare people. In the second verse of the Bible we read that "the earth was formless and empty, and darkness covered the deep waters. And the Spirit of God was hovering over the surface of the waters" (Genesis 1:2). The Holy Spirit hovered over the unformed earth like a cloud. Later, God's presence, like a cloud, led the Israelites in the desert (Exodus 13:21). We also read about a bright, shining cloud that came down when Jesus was on the top of a mountain with three of his disciples and that "a voice from the cloud said, 'This is my dearly loved Son, who brings me great joy. Listen to him'" (Matthew 17:5).

We get that same sense of an enveloping cloud of the presence of God when we read the words the angel said to Mary: "The Holy Spirit will come upon you, and the power of the Most High will overshadow you. So the baby to be born will be holy, and he will be called the Son of God" (Luke 1:35).

The angel said that the Holy Spirit would "come upon" Mary and "overshadow" her, similar to the way a cloud might. God, in the person of the Holy Spirit, would come over her and do a creative work in her womb, making new life.

While Mary's experience was certainly unique, we all desperately need the Holy Spirit to come upon us and overshadow us. We need him to make new life where there is deadness in our spirits, to bring light where there is darkness in our hearts. We need the Holy Spirit to enter into the chaos of our inner thoughts, emotions, and desires and change us from the inside out. We can't create new spiritual life on our own. We need the power of God to work inside us so that Christ can be born in us.

Jump for Joy

One of the most exciting times in a woman's pregnancy is when she begins to feel her child move inside her. It all becomes more real as the mother begins to feel the baby shift positions, move an arm or leg, or even hiccup.

When the angel told Zechariah that his wife, Elizabeth, would have a son named John who would prepare people to receive the Messiah, he said that this baby would be "filled with the Holy Spirit, even before his birth" (Luke 1:15). And when Elizabeth was six months pregnant, her relative Mary came to visit. When Mary, carrying Jesus in her womb, walked in, something amazing happened. Luke wrote:

> At the sound of Mary's greeting, Elizabeth's child leaped within her, and Elizabeth was filled with the Holy Spirit. Elizabeth gave a glad cry and exclaimed to Mary, "God has blessed you above all women, and your child is blessed. Why am I so honored, that the mother of my Lord should visit me? When I heard your greeting, the baby in my womb jumped for joy."
>
> LUKE 1:41-44

It must have taken Elizabeth's breath away when she sensed the growing baby in her belly have a physical response to Mary's walking toward her. Elizabeth could feel her baby's excitement, and she knew why he was excited. Luke said, "Elizabeth was filled with the Holy Spirit." Both mother and child were filled with the Holy Spirit, and the Spirit enabled them to sense the presence of the Messiah in Mary's womb.

The Holy Spirit helps us recognize that we need Jesus to save us. In fact, he's the only way we can respond to Jesus. We could never do it on our own. And when the Holy Spirit softens our hearts to welcome Jesus in, we, like the baby in Elizabeth's womb, jump for joy!

Magnification

As Mary thought through what the angel told her and considered how amazing it was that God had chosen her—an ordinary person—to be the human mother of God's Son, she broke out into a song: "Oh, how my soul praises the Lord. How my spirit rejoices in God my Savior! For he took notice of his lowly servant girl, and from now on all generations will call me blessed" (Luke 1:46-48).

Another Bible translation says that Mary said, "My soul *magnifies* the Lord" (NKJV, emphasis added). What did she mean by *magnifies*?

When you look at something through a magnifying glass, it looks much bigger than it actually is. Is that what Mary meant when she said, "My soul magnifies the Lord"? Was she trying to make God look bigger than he actually is?

We can never make God bigger or greater than he is. The truth is, we can never fully take in or understand God's greatness. But we can magnify him. We magnify God not by making him bigger than he truly is, but by making him greater in our thoughts, in our affections, in our memories, and in our expectations. We magnify him by having higher, larger, and truer thoughts of him. We magnify him by praising him and telling others about his greatness so they can have bigger thoughts about him too.

Sometimes we wonder why we aren't happy, why we make sinful choices, why we feel distant from God. Often it's because we have small thoughts about God and magnified thoughts of ourselves, our wants, our rights, our accomplishments. Mary, the one God chose to be the mother of his Son, could have easily allowed her thoughts of herself to become larger, even prideful. But instead of magnifying herself, she magnified the Lord.

Bethlehem's Baby

Bethlehem was a small and unimpressive village, but the prophet Micah had given an amazing prophecy about this little town. "You, O Bethlehem Ephrathah, are only a small village among all the people of Judah. Yet a ruler of Israel, whose origins are in the distant past, will come from you. . . . And he will stand to lead his flock with the LORD's strength" (Micah 5:2, 4).

It had been over four hundred years since Micah wrote this prophecy. The Jewish people knew this prophecy, and they knew that the Messiah would be a descendant of King David, who was from Bethlehem (1 Samuel 16:1). But even so, many people of Jesus' day were surprised that their Savior would be born as a baby in such a small, unremarkable village.

For some reason, people tend to be surprised when someone from a small town accomplishes something of true greatness. We have a tendency to think that for something or someone to be significant, the idea, the business, or the person must be born and raised in a major city or a well-known place and must be from a well-known or well-off family.

When God sent Jesus, he turned upside down every expectation of what people thought would make him great. Jesus came as a baby instead of a grown man. He was born to ordinary parents, not people of prominence or power. He came as a humble teacher rather than a conquering king. And he was born in an obscure little town rather than one of the great cities of the day.

This tells us something important about how God chooses the people he will use and bless. He doesn't choose on the basis of accomplishments or reputation or worldly value. God chooses to use simple, ordinary things and people so that he is the one who gets all the glory.

DECEMBER 13

Prepare the Way

What happens at your house when guests are coming? Do you clean up things that are messy, fix things that are broken, make plans for how you will welcome your visitors? As God prepared to send his Son into the world, he sent someone to get things ready. He had promised to do that, so some people were watching for this special individual.

Two Old Testament prophets (Malachi and Isaiah) had prophesied that before the Messiah would come, God would send a messenger to prepare the people. Malachi wrote, "Look! I am sending my messenger, and he will prepare the way before me. . . . Look, I am sending you the prophet Elijah" (Malachi 3:1; 4:5). Isaiah had written, "Listen! It's the voice of someone shouting, 'Clear the way through the wilderness for the LORD! Make a straight highway through the wasteland for our God!'" (Isaiah 40:3). Mark recorded, "This messenger was John the Baptist" (Mark 1:4). Luke wrote, "He will be a man with the spirit and power of Elijah. He will prepare the people for the coming of the Lord. He will turn the hearts of the fathers to their children, and he will cause those who are rebellious to accept the wisdom of the godly" (Luke 1:17).

John the Baptist was the person God sent to prepare his people for Jesus. It wasn't food or beds that needed to be prepared; it was hearts. It was John's mission to call people to repent—to leave behind their sin and turn back to God. John prepared the people for Jesus by helping them get their hearts ready to receive him.

God knows our hearts need to be prepared to receive Jesus. During December we tend to get very busy preparing for Christmas with parties and programs and presents. But the most important preparation we need to make is to prepare our hearts to welcome Jesus in a fresh, new way. We do this by cleaning out the clutter of sinful attitudes and selfishness so that we look expectantly for Jesus to make himself known to us.

DECEMBER 14

No Room for Him

Israel was an occupied country, and the people were forced to pay high taxes to the Roman emperor Caesar Augustus. To make sure he was getting as much in taxes as possible, Caesar took a census to count all the people living in every part of the empire, including Israel. All the people had to go to their ancestral hometowns to be counted. When all the people who were descendants of David arrived in the tiny town of Bethlehem to be counted, people made room in their houses for close relatives, and the places for travelers to stay filled up quickly. So when Mary and Joseph arrived in Bethlehem, the town was full so they had to nestle themselves into a place ordinarily used to house animals. While Mary and Joseph were in Bethlehem, "the time came for her baby to be born. She gave birth to her firstborn son. She . . . laid him in a manger, because there was no lodging available for them" (Luke 2:6-7).

We might think that since God could orchestrate an empire-wide census to bring Mary and Joseph to Bethlehem, surely he could have made sure there was a room available for Jesus to be born in. But somehow it seems appropriate that Jesus' life on earth would begin this way. Later Jesus said, "Foxes have dens to live in, and birds have nests, but the Son of Man has no place even to lay his head" (Matthew 8:20). Jesus never had a home of his own. His own people rejected him, and finally they crucified him because they refused to make room in their hearts to love and obey him.

Jesus never forces himself on us or into any area of our lives where we do not welcome him. So if we want Jesus to move in, we have to make room for him. We have to clear other things— even good things—out of our schedules if we want to make time to listen to him by reading his Word and talking to him through prayer. We have to make room in our thoughts for him, finding quiet times to focus on him, not just in this busy Christmas season, but all year long. When we open the door to Jesus and welcome him in, he makes himself at home in our hearts.

DECEMBER 15

Clothed in Humility

Most of us like to look good. We realize that what we wear sends a message about us, and we want other people to think well of us. So we look for clothes that will tell people what we want to say about who we are, where we've come from, and what is important to us.

Long before Jesus was born—before he even created the world—he existed with God in all his heavenly glory. But Jesus chose to leave heaven and his robes of glory. He laid them aside to be wrapped in rags.

Mary didn't have nice clothes to put on Jesus when he was born in Bethlehem. In fact, there were no clothes at all for him—just strips of cloth that were wrapped around him. Luke wrote, "She gave birth to her firstborn son. She wrapped him snugly in strips of cloth and laid him in a manger" (Luke 2:7). So from the day he was born, Jesus' clothing told us something significant about who he is and what he is like. The way he was dressed reflected the type of man he would grow up to be—humble and lowly.

We see something similar in another scene much later in Jesus' life. The night before he died, Jesus took off his robe and wrapped a towel around his waist. Then he began to wash the dusty feet of his disciples. This was "servant work," an act of deep humility and service. When Jesus finished, he told them, "I have given you an example to follow" (John 13:15). This is the way all those who are disciples of Jesus are called to dress—in the clothing of a humble servant.

Throughout his life and as he faced death, Jesus showed us what it looks like to clothe ourselves in humility—not only in terms of actual clothing but in the inner attitudes of our hearts. "He took the humble position of a slave" (Philippians 2:7) instead of seeking to impress. When we choose to clothe ourselves in this way, we reveal that we are not out to impress, but to serve.

DECEMBER 16

Good News of Great Joy

Some people think anything having to do with God is very serious and could never be outrageously happy. They assume that doing things for God, studying about God, going to church and worshiping God, or even just thinking about God will be really boring and no fun. But Jesus is not a bore or a burden; he's not a drag or drudgery. Jesus is the greatest joy in the universe! He's the best news anyone has ever heard! In fact, nothing in all the world can give people as much joy as Jesus can.

That's what the angel told the shepherds who were taking care of their sheep on that dark night outside Bethlehem. Luke recorded,

> Suddenly, an angel of the Lord appeared among them, and the radiance of the Lord's glory surrounded them. They were terrified, but the angel reassured them. "Don't be afraid!" he said. "I bring you good news that will bring great joy to all people. The Savior—yes, the Messiah, the Lord—has been born today in Bethlehem, the city of David!"
>
> LUKE 2:9-11

Initially, instead of being excited, the shepherds were afraid—terrified, even. Evidently the angel was right there with them and radiated a bright light like they had never seen, and it was scary.

But the good news of Jesus replaced their fear with joy. What was this good news? "The Savior—yes, the Messiah, the Lord—has been born today." The good news was that the Messiah the Jews had been expecting for centuries was born that very night.

When the shepherds checked it out for themselves, they found that what the angel had told them was true, so they returned to their flocks, "glorifying and praising God for all they had heard and seen" (Luke 2:20). They couldn't keep what they had seen to themselves. They told everyone what happened. "And all who heard it wondered at what the shepherds told them" (Luke 2:18, ESV). That word *wondered* means that the people who heard about it marveled—they were blown away.

The reason we celebrate Christmas is that we are *still* blown away by the incredible news that God became a baby that night in Bethlehem. And when we grow in our understanding of what this means, we begin to experience the great joy the angels talked about.

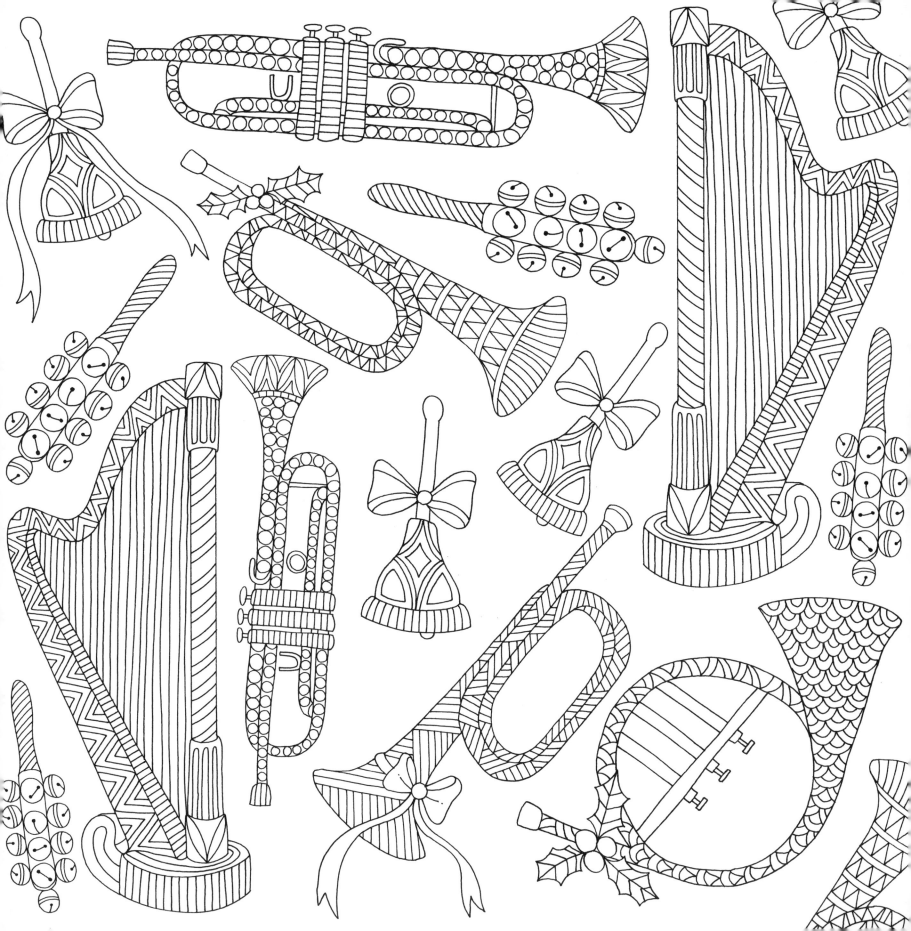

DECEMBER 17

Glory Revealed

Are there any wrapped packages under the Christmas tree at your house yet? Won't it be fun to tear off the paper so that what's inside will be revealed for everybody to see?

A long, long time before Jesus was born, the prophet Isaiah wrote, "The glory of the LORD will be revealed, and all people will see it together" (Isaiah 40:5). Like a present is unwrapped, revealing what is inside, Isaiah was saying that the glory of God would be "unwrapped" so that everyone could see what it really looked like.

What is the "glory of the LORD"? The glory of the Lord is the expression of who God is, the demonstration of his character. It is the beauty and brightness of God made visible. This is what happened that night so long ago when the shepherds were guarding their sheep. It seemed like an ordinary night—just like so many nights before out in the fields. But then, "suddenly, an angel of the Lord appeared among them, and the radiance of the Lord's glory surrounded them" (Luke 2:9).

God made his glory visible—in fact, it surrounded the shepherds. It was as if God pulled back the wrapping of the heavens so that God's glory spilled out and around those simple shepherds. What they saw was a glory that has always been there but is usually hidden from human view.

The writer to the Hebrews wrote that Jesus "*radiates* God's own glory and *expresses the very character of God*" (Hebrews 1:3, emphasis added). Glory is to God what brightness is to the sun. We "see" the sun by means of seeing its rays. The round ball of fire in the sky is the sun streaming forth in its radiance. Similarly, we see God the Father by seeing Jesus. Jesus is the radiance of God streaming down on us so we can see God and experience God and know God.

While God's people had seen glimpses of the glory of God before Jesus' birth, they had never seen it so clearly or so brightly. The birth of Christ was the revelation—or the unwrapping—of the glory of the Lord. By faith we too can see this glory. And the day will come when Christ will return and we will see his glory with our eyes.

DECEMBER 18

Peace on Earth

When the angel appeared to the shepherds to tell them about the Savior born in Bethlehem, he brought an army with him. But it wasn't an army of soldiers. Luke wrote, "Suddenly, the angel was joined by a vast host of others—the armies of heaven—praising God and saying, 'Glory to God in highest heaven, and peace on earth to those with whom God is pleased'" (Luke 2:13-14). The angel came with an army of angels.

Usually when we think about an army, we think of war, not peace, right? But that night heaven began to invade earth—not to fight against us or destroy us, but to save us. Isaiah prophesied that Jesus would be the "Prince of Peace," and that the peace he would bring would last forever (Isaiah 9:6-7). Jesus didn't come to destroy his enemies, but to make peace with them. He came to turn his enemies into friends.

We probably have never thought of ourselves as enemies of God. But the Bible says that whether we realize it or not, all of us, at one point, were God's enemies. Left on our own, we are sinners who naturally fight against God. That makes him our enemy. But God has not left us on our own. Even though we have declared war on him deep in our hearts, he has declared peace with us. This friendship is made possible not because Jesus was born, but because Jesus would die. Paul wrote, "Since our friendship with God was restored by the death of his Son while we were still his enemies, we will certainly be saved through the life of his Son" (Romans 5:10).

God does not want to wage war against us even though we've been rebellious toward him. Instead, he has reached out to us, making the first move toward peace. He gives us the grace to overcome our natural resistance toward him so that we can develop a deep friendship with him. He gives us the faith to trust in him, making us one of "those with whom God is pleased."

DECEMBER 19

He Became Poor

Who has asked you what you want for Christmas this year? Since we are asked this question from an early age, it is easy for Christmas to become all about *getting* rather than *giving*. Wouldn't a better question to ask each other be, "What are you *giving* for Christmas?" Giving is what Christmas is all about, and we see that when we look at what Jesus did in coming to earth. He did not come to get something from us, but to give us everything that has real and lasting value.

God made the universe. Long before God the Son came to earth, everything was his. The glory and joy of heaven were his. The power and privilege of heaven were his. In heaven he was rich in his relationship with his Father and the Spirit. But to come to earth, he left it all behind. Paul wrote, "You know the generous grace of our Lord Jesus Christ. Though he was rich, yet for your sakes he became poor, so that by his poverty he could make you rich" (2 Corinthians 8:9).

Jesus gave up the riches of heaven to become a poor carpenter on earth. He gave up his close relationship with his Father when he took our sin upon himself on the cross. In this way, he became poor so that we could become rich. Not wealthy, but rich spiritually. Because he became poor, we can enjoy the richness of a satisfying, saving relationship with God forever.

These riches are available, however, only to those who recognize how poor they are apart from Christ. He does not give his riches to people who think they are already good enough for God and who are satisfied with what they have in this world. Jesus said, "God blesses those who are poor and realize their need for him" (Matthew 5:3).

It is seeing this generosity of Jesus that turns selfish people into joyful givers. We tend toward selfishness because we believe the lie that keeping more for ourselves will make us happy. But Jesus shows us that what will truly make us happy is to become generous givers—like he is.

DECEMBER 20

Seeing and Believing

*T*hink about a time when someone told you something that seemed so incredible you said, "I will have to see it to believe it." It must have been that sense of amazement and curiosity that caused the shepherds to hurry to Bethlehem. Luke wrote:

> When the angels had returned to heaven, the shepherds said to each other, "Let's go to Bethlehem! Let's see this thing that has happened, which the Lord has told us about." They hurried to the village and found Mary and Joseph. And there was the baby, lying in the manger. After seeing him, the shepherds told everyone what had happened and what the angel had said to them about this child.
>
> LUKE 2:15-17

Don't you wish there had been a modern-day news crew on the scene so we could see what the shepherds saw? While we see pretty Christmas cards drawn of this scene with a glow around the baby and his mother, the truth is that the baby Jesus looked like an ordinary infant, and his parents like ordinary people. The shepherds believed what the angels told them about this ordinary-looking baby, and because they believed, the baby became their Savior. Their lives were never the same after seeing and believing in Jesus.

But it must have been difficult for them when they "told everyone what had happened and what the angel had said to them about this child" (Luke 2:17). Apparently "all who heard the shepherds' story were astonished" (Luke 2:18). The story the shepherds told was so amazing and unusual, many must have found it hard to believe. Some people probably said, "That sounds crazy." Some people probably shrugged their shoulders, saying, "That's interesting, but I don't need anybody to save me—especially a baby." But others believed that Jesus was the one God promised to send so long ago, and because they believed, their lives were completely changed.

We all have the same choice to make when we hear the astonishing news that God became a baby and that he is the only Savior. Our reaction to this astonishing news is all-important. Will we shrug our shoulders in disbelief, or will we bend our knees and believe in our hearts?

A Birthday Present for Jesus

Most of us have a little list going this time of year—if not on paper, then in our heads. It's that list of what we're hoping someone might give us for Christmas. But isn't it interesting that at Christmas *we* get gifts on someone *else's* birthday? Jesus is the real birthday boy. Have you ever thought about what Jesus might want for his birthday this Christmas?

The Bible tells us that after Jesus was born, "some wise men from eastern lands arrived in Jerusalem, asking, 'Where is the newborn king of the Jews? We saw his star as it rose, and we have come to worship him'" (Matthew 2:1-2).

An unusual star in the sky led these men to Jesus. Matthew wrote that "when they saw the star, they rejoiced *exceedingly with great joy*" (Matthew 2:10, NASB, emphasis added). It's almost as if there aren't enough words to express how much joy they felt over this star that would lead them to Jesus.

When the wise men saw Jesus, they bowed down and worshiped him. And they gave him expensive gifts. Giving is part of worship. If we really admire and love the one we are worshiping, we are glad to give ourselves, and whatever we have of value, to him. If Christ is the true object of our worship, then no one has to force us to worship him or give of ourselves to him. It is what we want to do.

Since it is Jesus' birthday that we celebrate at Christmas, perhaps you should consider what *you* could give to Jesus for his birthday present. Perhaps the gift you could give to Jesus this Christmas is to say to him from your heart, "I'm so happy you brought me to you! You are worthy of my worship, and I want you to be the King of my life. You are more precious to me than anything I own, and I gladly give you the honor you deserve." That is a gift he will enjoy.

42

MY BIRTHDAY GIFTS TO *Jesus*

DECEMBER 22

Born to Die

When a baby is born, people usually celebrate and talk about the long life ahead for that child. But from his birth—even before his birth—a cloud of death loomed over the baby Jesus. This was a baby who was born to die.

The wise men who followed the star to find Jesus seemed to know some things about the Old Testament prophecies about the Messiah. When they came to see Jesus, they actually fulfilled one of those prophecies. Isaiah had written about the Messiah, "Mighty kings will come to see your radiance. . . . [They] will bring gold and frankincense and will come worshiping the LORD" (Isaiah 60:3, 6). Matthew recorded that the wise men "entered the house and saw the child with his mother, Mary, and . . . they opened their treasure chests and gave him gifts of gold, frankincense, and myrrh" (Matthew 2:11).

Gold, frankincense, and myrrh are certainly unusual gifts for a baby! Gold was a gift suited to a king. The wise men must have recognized Jesus as King and so they brought him gold and bowed down to him. Frankincense was a perfume mixed with ground wheat or barley for the grain offering. Frankincense gave off an aroma that was pleasing to God as it burned. This, too, was an appropriate gift for Jesus, who in his life, but especially in his death, would be a pleasing sacrifice to God.

The third gift the wise men brought to Jesus was especially unusual. Myrrh is a sweet-smelling substance that was used to preserve dead bodies and overcome the smell of decay. Why give myrrh to a baby? Perhaps the wise men also understood Isaiah's prophecy that "it was the LORD's good plan to crush him and cause him grief. Yet when his life is made an offering for sin, he will have many descendants" (Isaiah 53:10). The Messiah came as a baby for the very purpose of dying as a sacrifice for sin.

Because Jesus was born to die, we don't have to be afraid of death. Yes, we will all die someday. But if we belong to Jesus, he will one day resurrect our dead bodies and make them new so that we will live with him forever.

A Real Hero

When you're really in trouble, you want someone strong to show up to save you—a real hero. And as people living in this world, we are really in trouble, really in need of someone who can save us from our slavery to sin. God sent someone to save us. The prophet Isaiah wrote about him:

> For a child is born to us, a son is given to us. The government will rest on his shoulders. And he will be called: Wonderful Counselor, Mighty God, Everlasting Father, Prince of Peace. His government and its peace will never end. He will rule with fairness and justice from the throne of his ancestor David for all eternity. The passionate commitment of the LORD of Heaven's Armies will make this happen!
>
> ISAIAH 9:6-7

God sent us a Savior in the form of a baby. The prophet Isaiah assured us, however, that Jesus would be no ordinary baby and that he would grow up to be no ordinary man.

As the Wonderful Counselor, he has the best ideas and strategies; he's the wisest and most perfect teacher. If we listen to him, we'll know what to do.

As the Mighty God, he uses his power on our behalf, helping us overcome sin. We can find protection in him when we're tempted.

As the Everlasting Father, he cares for us lovingly, with affection that has no limits. We can entrust ourselves to him.

As the Prince of Peace, he invites us into his Kingdom of full and perfect happiness, giving us the assurance of safety and security. As we submit to him, we will live lives of blessed closeness to him.

The child born to us became our strong deliverer and our source of security and satisfaction forever. The Son given *to* us gave himself *for* us.

Wonderful COUNSELOR,
Mighty GOD,
Everlasting FATHER,
PRINCE OF PEACE

Christmas Eve Scripture Reading

From the Gospel of Matthew, chapter 1:

This is how Jesus the Messiah was born. His mother, Mary, was engaged to be married to Joseph. But before the marriage took place, while she was still a virgin, she became pregnant through the power of the Holy Spirit. Joseph, to whom she was engaged, was a righteous man and did not want to disgrace her publicly, so he decided to break the engagement quietly.

As he considered this, an angel of the Lord appeared to him in a dream. "Joseph, son of David," the angel said, "do not be afraid to take Mary as your wife. For the child within her was conceived by the Holy Spirit. And she will have a son, and you are to name him Jesus, for he will save his people from their sins."

All of this occurred to fulfill the Lord's message through his prophet:

"Look! The virgin will conceive a child!
    She will give birth to a son,
and they will call him Immanuel,
    which means 'God is with us.'"

When Joseph woke up, he did as the angel of the Lord commanded and took Mary as his wife. But he did not have sexual relations with her until her son was born. And Joseph named him Jesus. (verses 18-25)

Christmas Day Scripture Reading

From the Gospel of Luke, chapter 2:

At that time the Roman emperor, Augustus, decreed that a census should be taken throughout the Roman Empire. (This was the first census taken when Quirinius was governor of Syria.) All returned to their own ancestral towns to register for this census. And because Joseph was a descendant of King David, he had to go to Bethlehem in Judea, David's ancient home. He traveled there from the village of Nazareth in Galilee. He took with him Mary, to whom he was engaged, who was now expecting a child.

And while they were there, the time came for her baby to be born. She gave birth to her firstborn son. She wrapped him snugly in strips of cloth and laid him in a manger, because there was no lodging available for them.

That night there were shepherds staying in the fields nearby, guarding their flocks of sheep. Suddenly, an angel of the Lord appeared among them, and the radiance of the Lord's glory surrounded them. They were terrified, but the angel reassured them. "Don't be afraid!" he said. "I bring you good news that will bring great joy to all people. The Savior—yes, the Messiah, the Lord—has been born today in Bethlehem, the city of David! And you will recognize him by this sign: You will find a baby wrapped snugly in strips of cloth, lying in a manger."

Suddenly, the angel was joined by a vast host of others—the armies of heaven—praising God and saying,

"Glory to God in highest heaven,
 and peace on earth to those with whom God is pleased."

When the angels had returned to heaven, the shepherds said to each other, "Let's go to Bethlehem! Let's see this thing that has happened, which the Lord has told us about."

They hurried to the village and found Mary and Joseph. And there was the baby, lying in the manger. After seeing him, the shepherds told everyone what had happened and what the angel had said to them about this child. All who heard the shepherds' story were astonished, but Mary kept all these things in her heart and thought about them often. The shepherds went back to their flocks, glorifying and praising God for all they had heard and seen. It was just as the angel had told them. (verses 1-20)

The Greatest Gift

What's the best gift you received this Christmas? You can hardly wait to play with it, put it on, or figure it out! When we receive a gift that pleases us, we want to enjoy it and share it with others.

God is the most generous Giver in the universe, and he has given us the most valuable gift in the universe—Jesus himself. John wrote, "From his abundance we have all received one gracious blessing after another" (John 1:16). God knows just what to give us, just what we need most, and that is Jesus. It is the greatness of this gift that prompts us to give each other gifts at Christmas.

But some people don't realize how beautiful and valuable the gift of Jesus is, and so they never truly receive him.

Sometimes we are given a gift that we think is not really useful to us, and therefore we never take it out of the box. We stash it away in a closet or on a shelf somewhere in case we need it someday. Sadly, that's what some people do in regard to Jesus. They want to keep him handy for when something comes along that they can't handle on their own, but for now they have no interest in making him part of their day-to-day lives, and so they put him on the shelf. They simply don't believe he is as good as the Bible says he is, and so they have no real or lasting joy in having received this great gift.

John wrote, "To all who received him, to those who believed in his name, he gave the right to become children of God" (John 1:12, NIV). God has given us the gift of Jesus, but it is up to each of us to receive that gift, unwrap that gift, make that gift a part of our daily lives. To receive Christ is to recognize that he is the most beautiful, most desirable treasure in the universe and open up our lives to him, saying, "I must have him!"

DECEMBER 27

Eagerly Waiting

It's hard to wait—especially when you really want something and you've been disappointed over and over while waiting for it. Sometimes disappointment makes you want to give up and stop wanting it so much. That's what many people did before Jesus came—they gave up waiting for and wanting a messiah to come and deliver them. They got tired of the wait, so they stopped looking and longing. They stopped expecting that God would fulfill his promise.

But not everybody got tired of waiting. Luke 2 tells about two people—Simeon and Anna—who were still eagerly waiting and watching for the promised Messiah. Simeon was a righteous man who lived in Jerusalem, and God had promised him that he would not die before seeing the Messiah. When Mary and Joseph brought the baby Jesus to the Temple, Simeon took Jesus in his arms and said,

> "Sovereign Lord, now let your servant die in peace,
>   as you have promised.
> I have seen your salvation,
>   which you have prepared for all people.
> He is a light to reveal God to the nations,
>   and he is the glory of your people Israel!"

Anna was an eighty-four-year-old widow who spent her time fasting and praying at the Temple. After hearing Simeon's words about Jesus, she also began praising God, and she spread the news to others who had been waiting for the Messiah to come.

When Simeon saw the baby Jesus, he knew the wait was over. And when Anna heard what Simeon said, she shared it with everyone else she knew who was waiting expectantly.

Once again we are in a period of waiting—waiting for Jesus to come a second time. And we can expect that, like the first time, Jesus will be revealed to those who are waiting eagerly to see him. It might seem like it will never happen, and the world thinks it's ridiculous to be looking for Jesus' arrival. But we continue waiting and watching.

54

Thinking It Over

Pretty soon it will be time to take down the Christmas lights and put away the decorations. January will be here, and this Christmas will be a memory. If we're not careful, ordinary life can cause us to lose our sense of wonder over Jesus' coming.

That might have happened on the first Christmas, too. Though it seems like everyone would have kept their eyes on a baby whose birth had been announced by a sky full of angels, evidently people lost interest. The shepherds had to go back to taking care of their sheep. The wise men went back to their own country. It seems most people set aside their hopes that this baby could make a difference in the world.

"All who heard the shepherds' story were astonished, but Mary kept all these things in her heart and thought about them often" (Luke 2:18-19). Other translations say that Mary "pondered" all the things she heard and experienced. Though most people who witnessed what happened in Bethlehem may have put it in the back of their minds or out of their minds, Mary continued to really think it over. It was as if she said to herself, "I won't forget hearing the angel. I will remember what it was like to have the Holy Spirit come over me; I will keep the memory close of seeing Jesus worshiped by the wise men."

Though Mary certainly knew this was a child God had given her, and the song she sang celebrated that this baby would be the fulfillment of God's promises to Abraham, evidently she didn't understand everything about Jesus and what he came to do—but she wanted to. So Mary began a process of "connecting the dots" in her own mind, adding up the prophecies about the Messiah from the Old Testament prophets that her son, Jesus, fulfilled at his birth. She must have marveled at this child of hers who never gave in to temptation and seemed to understand the purpose for his life at such a young age. She must have wondered how and when her son would begin to turn the world upside down and how it would impact her entire family.

While others lost interest, Mary thought through everything about who Jesus was, why he came, and what he would accomplish. She thought through what the angel had said to her and to Joseph about Jesus, the song God had given to her, the visits of the shepherds and the wise men. Mary is a good example for us—especially those of us who have heard the Christmas story so many times that we are hardly startled by its startling aspects. We have to think it through, meditating on what it tells us about Jesus, whom God sent to save us.

DECEMBER 29

The Word Became Human

*I*t can be fun to dress up as something we are not. When we put on costumes, it is usually for a brief time, and then we take off the costume and go back to being who we really are. Just because we dress up like a character in a movie or a person from history doesn't mean we actually *become* that character or person.

We might assume that Jesus put on a "costume" of skin to be a human for the thirty-three years he spent on this earth, and then he went back to his "usual" self when he returned to heaven. But Jesus went much further than that. John wrote, "The Word *became* human" (John 1:14, emphasis added). Jesus *became* flesh—forever. He didn't just appear to be human; he *became* human—not just for his brief life on earth, but for all eternity. Even now, Jesus is in heaven at the right hand of God in his post-resurrection, glorified, human body.

Jesus was willing to be human in all its messiness. The Son of God had to let Mary change his diaper. He went through puberty. He was susceptible to disease and had surging hormones. Jesus got hungry and sleepy, his muscles ached after a hard day working in the carpenter's shop, his nose got sunburned, and his lips got chapped.

Jesus became absolutely human, not just in body, but in mind. Jesus went to school as a child. And he didn't sit in the front row with all the answers automatically programmed into him. The Bible says that Jesus learned just like we do: "Jesus grew in wisdom and in stature" (Luke 2:52).

Jesus was also fully human in his emotions. He felt the range of human emotions that we feel. When Lazarus died, Jesus "was deeply moved in spirit and troubled" (John 11:33, NIV). He experienced joy (John 15:11), anger (Mark 3:5), and even surprise (Mark 6:6; Luke 7:9).

While we had no choice about being made of flesh and blood, Jesus chose to be human. While still being completely divine and completely holy, he also willingly took hold of the messiness of being a person. He entered into our reality, walking, breathing, and living in our world. The only thing he did not do is sin. But the most important experience he went through as a human was physical death. This was his ultimate purpose in becoming flesh—so he could die in our place.

58

His Two Comings

The Old Testament prophets who wrote about the Messiah's coming saw his coming kind of like we see a range of mountains from far away. They wrote about things that would happen and things the Messiah would do when he came. But from so far away, they couldn't understand that Christ would accomplish some of those things the first time he came and others when he comes again, at a time even further in the future. The prophets couldn't see the immense distances of time that separate one event from another. While being a prophet meant that you had a message from God, it didn't mean you always understood the meaning or the timing of the events predicted.

For example, the prophet Isaiah described the Messiah coming as a child who would be born (Isaiah 9:6), as a servant who would suffer (Isaiah 53), and as a lamb who would be led to the slaughter (Isaiah 53:7). These prophecies were clearly fulfilled by Jesus when he came the first time. But Isaiah also wrote that when the Messiah comes, "the wolf and the lamb will live together" (Isaiah 11:6) and that "he will rule with a powerful arm" (Isaiah 40:10). Isaiah prophesied about a day when "no longer will you need the sun to shine by day, nor the moon to give its light by night, for the LORD your God will be your everlasting light, and your God will be your glory" (Isaiah 60:19). Obviously these prophecies were not fulfilled when Christ came the first time. These are the things we look forward to when he will come the second time.

Many of the Old Testament prophecies about the Messiah are still awaiting fulfillment. So just as the people of Israel longed for the Messiah to come, we long for him to come again. Added to the Old Testament prophecies are all the things Jesus told us about his return—he said the whole world will see his coming on the clouds of heaven with great glory at a time when we least expect it. So Jesus said we must be ready all the time for his return. We don't know *when* it will be, but we know it will be.

DECEMBER 31

One Thing

*A*s the year comes to a close and we prepare to begin a new year, we know that our family will get busy doing lots of things—many good things. The new beginning that comes with a new year allows us to step back and consider if all the things that we are busy with help us move forward toward what is most important. We want to ask, Are the things we're doing helping us or hindering us from making progress in the one thing that is most important—the one thing that will matter for eternity?

Paul was determined to make sure that everything he was doing helped him in accomplishing the *one thing* that was most important. "I press on to possess that perfection for which Christ Jesus first possessed me," he said. "I focus on this one thing: Forgetting the past and looking forward to what lies ahead, I press on to reach the end of the race and receive the heavenly prize for which God, through Christ Jesus, is calling us" (Philippians 3:12-14). As Paul looked toward the future, he was determined to "press on." He wanted to continue to make progress in the life of faith—to love and trust God more tomorrow than he did yesterday. He wanted to live his life now in light of eternity. He didn't want to become distracted by anything that would steal his attention from what will matter for eternity.

What would it look like to "press on" toward knowing and enjoying Christ as you and your family enter another year? The kind of straining forward Paul wrote about means implementing the self-discipline and self-denial of a serious athlete. It means making plans and setting goals for ourselves in the areas of worship, studying God's Word, developing our prayer lives, and sharing Christ, so that by next year at this time we will be closer to Jesus.

Today is a good day to look back, look forward, and look inward. We want to see ourselves and our lives as Christ sees us and be willing to face hard truths about ourselves. But more important than looking inward is looking upward to Christ. Looking to Christ gives us a goal to pursue, a person to enjoy, a passion to feed. Looking to Christ orients the direction of the coming year—and of our entire lives.

Family Activities:
Conversation Starters
and
Coloring Pages

While the Advent season is a good time for individual reflection, it's also a good time to instill in the children we love a sense of anticipation for the coming of Jesus. The following pages include discussion questions and kid-friendly coloring pages for you and your young ones to work through as you consider together the significance of the coming of Christ into our world. Some pages were even created to be colored and cut out—bookmarks and ornaments to remind you of the season, wherever you are. My hope is that as you spend some time with the children in your world coloring and talking, you'll be able to help them escape our culture's consumer approach to Christmas and instead spark a sense of gratitude for Christ's first coming and anticipation for when he comes again.

THE SPIRIT OF GIVING

It is more blessed to give than to receive.
    Acts 20:35

Discussion Starters

What do you find yourself dreaming of getting? What do you find yourself dreaming of giving?

When have you experienced or observed someone else enjoying the happiness that comes from outrageous giving?

This Christmas, how can our family avoid the trap of making Christmas only about getting stuff?

Prayer

Generous, giving God, we want to put your word to the test this Christmas. We want to find out for ourselves how happy it will make us to give. We want to become generous givers like you are, confident that you will take care of all our needs.

AT HOME WITH JESUS

So the Word became human and made his home among us.
John 1:14

Discussion Starters

When someone wants to sit by you at an event or spend the night at your house, what does that say about how that person feels about you?

John describes God in the flesh as "full of unfailing love and faithfulness" (John 1:14). Do you think that is how most people see Jesus?

What difference would it make if our family lived as if Jesus had made himself "at home" in our house?

Prayer

You have come, Jesus, to make your home among us. And we welcome you! We believe you. We accept you. Make yourself at home in our home.

Faith to Believe

Gabriel appeared to her and said, "Greetings, favored woman! The Lord is with you!"
Confused and disturbed, Mary tried to think what the angel could mean. "Don't be afraid,
Mary," the angel told her, "for you have found favor with God!"
    Luke 1:28-30

Discussion Starters

What thoughts do you think went through Mary's mind when the angel was speaking to her?

What did Mary believe about God and his promises that allowed her to respond with a song of praise?

What difficult things has God asked our family to do or endure? How might these difficult things be God's gifts to us?

Prayer

God, give us faith to surrender ourselves to you even in the hard places of life. We want to be your servants. We believe that anything you ask of us will be good and right because you love us. Fill us with faith to trust you with whatever you ask of us.

JUMP FOR JOY

At the sound of Mary's greeting, Elizabeth's child leaped within her, and Elizabeth was filled with the Holy Spirit. Elizabeth gave a glad cry and exclaimed to Mary, "God has blessed you above all women, and your child is blessed. Why am I so honored, that the mother of my Lord should visit me? When I heard your greeting, the baby in my womb jumped for joy."
     Luke 1:41-44

Discussion Starters

Describe a time when you have been so happy and excited that you jumped for joy (or wished you could have).

What do you think the conversations between Elizabeth and Mary would have been like when Mary came to visit?

What other examples can you think of from the Bible when the Spirit gave someone the ability to recognize who Jesus was?

Prayer

Lord, fill us with your Spirit so that throughout this Christmas season we will jump for joy at your coming.

EXTRAORDINARY LOVE

You, O Bethlehem Ephrathah, are only a small village among all the people of Judah. Yet a ruler of Israel, whose origins are in the distant past, will come from you. . . . And he will stand to lead his flock with the Lord's strength.
    Micah 5:2, 4

Discussion Starters

Think of someone famous you know or have read about who came from a small town.

What are some of the ways we show that we believe bigger is better?

Bethlehem means "house of bread," and it was King David's hometown. Why are these two facts significant for the place of Jesus' birth?

Prayer

Child of Bethlehem, we are grateful to know that you came to ordinary people in an ordinary place, because we are ordinary. May your glory shine bright in this ordinary place we call home.

A HEART FOR JESUS

He will be a man with the spirit and power of Elijah. He will prepare the people for the coming of the Lord. He will turn the hearts of the fathers to their children, and he will cause those who are rebellious to accept the wisdom of the godly.
  Luke 1:17

Discussion Starters

When Luke said that John came with the "spirit and power of Elijah," he meant that John proclaimed judgment for sin and called for repentance. How does an awareness of our sin help prepare us for Jesus?

What happens when we refuse or neglect to prepare the way for Jesus to come to us?

As we think about what we do to prepare for company, what similar things can we do to prepare to welcome Jesus into our home this Christmas?

Prayer

Right now, Lord Jesus, our hearts are being prepared to receive you. Show us what must be removed, the sin that must be repented of, so that our hearts can fully receive you.

A Place for Jesus

And while they were there, the time came for her baby to be born. She gave birth to her firstborn son. She . . . laid him in a manger, because there was no lodging available for them.
      Luke 2:6-7

Discussion Starters

When Mary and Joseph arrived in Bethlehem, the town was so full they had to stay in a place used to house animals. What do you think it would be like to spend the night sleeping where animals are kept?

Why do you think Jesus lived a life of poverty rather than one of comfort and financial means?

What would it mean to make more room for Jesus in our schedules, our hearts, our home?

Prayer

Jesus, we want to make room for you in our home and in our hearts, and we know that doing so may mean changing our schedules or changing our habits. Show us what needs to be moved out so there will be plenty of room for you to dwell here with us.

Good News

Suddenly, an angel of the Lord appeared among them, and the radiance of the Lord's glory surrounded them. They were terrified, but the angel reassured them. "Don't be afraid!" he said. "I bring you good news that will bring great joy to all people. The Savior— yes, the Messiah, the Lord—has been born today in Bethlehem, the city of David!"
    Luke 2:9-11

Discussion Starters

What do you think it would be like to see an angel?

What made the coming of Jesus such good news for "all people"?

Do you think it is sometimes hard to be filled with joy at the Good News of Jesus? Why is that?

Prayer

We hear the good news about you, Jesus. Help us to see how good it is so we can experience the joy of your coming.

THE GLORY OF OUR GOD

The glory of the LORD will be revealed, and all people will see it together.
  Isaiah 40:5

Discussion Starters

Luke wrote that the shepherds were terrified when God's glory was revealed. What might have made it so scary?

Why do you think God's glory is usually hidden from human view?

Read 2 Corinthians 3:18. Where is the glory of God being revealed, and what does that mean?

Prayer

Give us eyes to see your glory, God, as we focus on who Jesus is and what he did for us.

WORTHY OF WORSHIP

Jesus was born in Bethlehem in Judea, during the reign of King Herod. About that time some wise men from eastern lands arrived in Jerusalem, asking, "Where is the newborn king of the Jews? We saw his star as it rose, and we have come to worship him."
    Matthew 2:1-2

Discussion Starters

Instead of thinking only about what you want to get this Christmas, what gifts would you like to *give*?

What does it mean to "worship" something or someone?

What gift could you give to Jesus this Christmas that would make him happy? And would it make you happy to give it to him?

Prayer

We seek after you and bow before you, Jesus. You are worthy of our worship. We give ourselves and our worship as our gifts to you.

THE GIFT OF JESUS

To all who received him, to those who believed in his name, he gave the right to become children of God.
    John 1:12, NIV

Discussion Starters

What are some of your favorite gifts that you've received? How do these gifts show that the people who gave them knew what you wanted or needed?

How have you enjoyed the generosity of God over this past year?

Romans 8:32 says, "Since [God] did not spare even his own Son but gave him up for us all, won't he also give us everything else?" How does this verse encourage you as you think about needs you have in the coming year?

Prayer

Jesus, we receive you! We welcome you into our home and into our hearts this Christmas. Show us what it means to unwrap this incredible gift we've been given and put you at the very center of our day-to-day lives.

Jesus, Our Friend

Because God's children are human beings—made of flesh and blood—the Son also became flesh and blood. For only as a human being could he die, and only by dying could he break the power of the devil, who had the power of death.
Hebrews 2:14

Discussion Starters

Think about Jesus as a baby and as a young child and teenager. What human things must he have experienced?

As you consider some of the things that are hard about being human, how does it help to know that Jesus understands because he is human too?

Jesus not only lived as a human but also died and was resurrected as a human. How does that give us hope?

Prayer

Because you became human, Jesus, you understand our struggles. And because, as a human, you died and rose again, we can be confident that we will too!

Also by Nancy Guthrie

BOOKS

Holding On to Hope

The One Year Book of Hope

Hearing Jesus Speak into Your Sorrow

When Your Family's Lost a Loved One (with David Guthrie)

What Grieving People Wish You Knew about What Really Helps (and What Really Hurts)

One Year of Dinner Table Devotions and Discussion Starters

The One Year Book of Discovering Jesus in the Old Testament

Abundant Life in Jesus

BIBLE STUDIES

Hoping for Something Better

The Promised One

The Lamb of God

The Son of David

The Wisdom of God

The Word of the Lord

About the Author and Artist

Nancy Guthrie lives in Nashville, Tennessee. She speaks at conferences around the country and internationally and is currently pursuing graduate studies at Reformed Theological Seminary. She and her husband, David, are the co-hosts of the GriefShare video series used in more than 10,000 churches around the world, and they host Respite Retreats for couples who have faced the death of a child. She is the author of numerous books, including *Holding On to Hope, Abundant Life in Jesus,* and *The One Year Book of Discovering Jesus in the Old Testament.* She also hosts the *Help Me Teach the Bible* podcast at The Gospel Coalition.

Lizzie Preston is a designer, illustrator, and all-around creative who was born and bred in Birmingham, United Kingdom. After receiving a bachelor's degree in graphic design from Nottingham Trent University, she worked for six years at a commercial greeting card company. Lizzie loves exploring new styles of design, from doodles to laser cuts, graphic to hand drawn, and she has a passion for typography and surface patterns.

Has your family enjoyed talking together about truths from God's Word each day during December? Why not keep it up all year through? *One Year of Dinner Table Devotions and Discussion Starters* by Nancy Guthrie serves up daily truths from God's Word to chew on and apply to real life at a level that kids from elementary age through high school will understand and relate to. Transform family devotions from dry lectures into dynamic conversations as you draw closer to each other—and closer to God himself.

LIVING
EXPRESSIONS™
COLLECTION

978-1-4964-1406-9

978-1-4964-1579-0

RESTORE MY SOUL

Grab your colored pencils and get ready to refresh your spirit. Both contemplative and imaginative, *Restore My Soul* includes short reflections on Scripture and intricate illustrations created for meditation and prayer.

GRATITUDE

Bring creative journaling and coloring into your personal time with God with this prayer and praise book! Filled with over 100 designs to color, plenty of space for journaling and sketching, and 40 prayers, *Gratitude* helps you express your devotion to God with your whole heart!

CP1097